Contar: De cinco en cinco
Counting by: Fives

Esther Sarfatti

Rourke

Rourke Publishing LLC
Vero Beach, Florida 32964

www.rourkepublishing.com

PHOTO CREDITS: © Scott Waite: page 3; © Renee Brady: page 5; © Joe Cicak: page 7; © Sandra O'Claire: page 9; © Sean Locke: page 13; © Pathathai Chungyam: page 15; © Jim Jurica: page 17; © Dave Logan: page 19; © BTina Rencelj: page 21; © Denise Crew: page 23.

Editor: Robert Stengard-Olliges

Cover design by Nicola Stratford.

Library of Congress Cataloging-in-Publication Data

Sarfatti, Esther.
  [Counting by fives. Spanish]
  Contar de cinco en cinco / Esther Sarfatti.
      p. cm. -- (Conceptos)
  ISBN 978-1-60044-747-1
  1. Counting--Juvenile literature. I. Title.

Printed in the USA

CG/CG

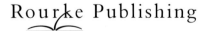

Rourke Publishing

www.rourkepublishing.com – rourke@rourkepublishing.com
Post Office Box 3328, Vero Beach, FL 32964

Aquí hay cinco.
This is five.

¿Cuántos grupos de cinco puedes encontrar?

How many groups of five can you find?

cinco 5

5 Five

five cinco

5

Una estrella de mar tiene cinco brazos.

A starfish has five arms.

7

Un pie tiene cinco dedos.

A foot has five toes.

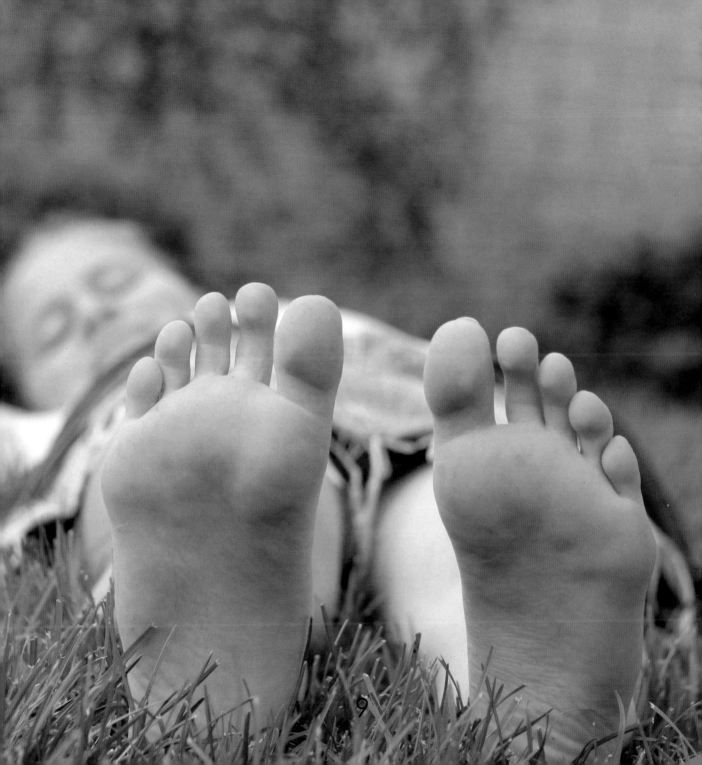

Un pentágono tiene
cinco lados.

A pentagon has five sides.

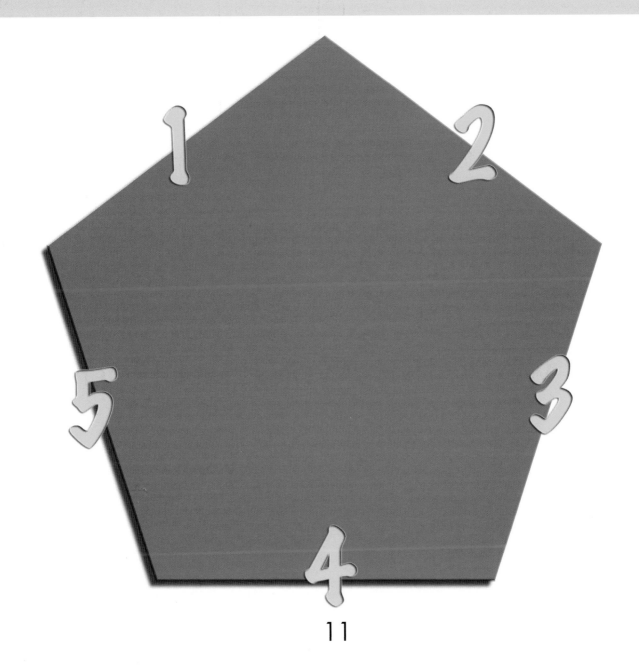

11

Una semana tiene cinco
días escolares.

A week has five school days.

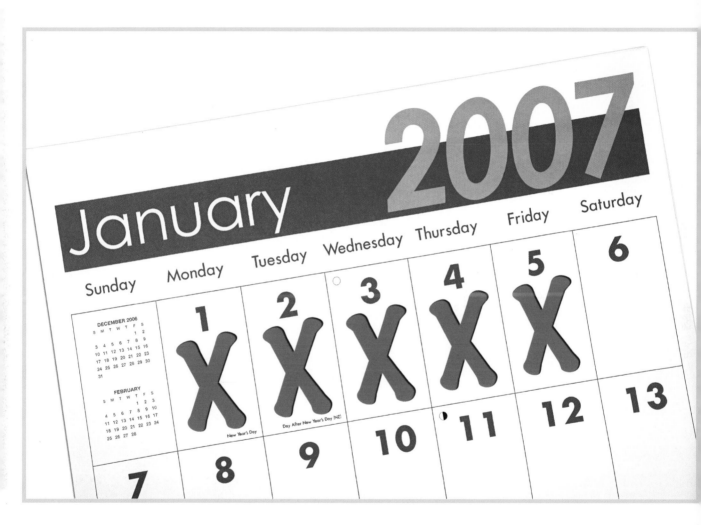

Estas son cinco niñas y cinco paletas.

These are five girls and five popsicles.

Este pastel tiene cinco velas.

This cake has five candles.

Estas estrellas tienen cinco puntas.

These stars have five points.

1

5 2

4 3

Estos son cinco perros.

These are five dogs.

Estos cinco niños
están jugando.
¡Es divertido contar de cinco
en cinco!

These five kids are playing.
Counting by fives is fun!

Índice

Index

Lecturas adicionales / Further Reading

Dahl, Michael. *Lots of Ladybugs: Counting by Fives*. Picture Window Books, 2005.

Dahl, Michael. *Hands Down: Counting by Fives*. Picture Window Books, 2006.

Páginas Web recomendadas / Recommended Websites

www.edhelper.com/kindergarten/Number_5.htm

www.enchantedlearning.com/languagebooks/spanish/numbers/

Acerca de la autora / About the Author

Esther Sarfatti lleva más de 15 años trabajando con libros infantiles como editora y traductora. Ésta es su primera serie como autora. Nacida en Brooklyn, Nueva York, donde creció en una familia trilingüe, Esther vive actualmente en Madrid, España, con su esposo y su hijo.

Esther Sarfatti has worked with children's books for over 15 years as an editor and translator. This is her first series as an author. Born in Brooklyn, New York, and brought up in a trilingual home, Esther currently lives with her husband and son in Madrid, Spain.

10/08